WHISTLING IN THE

DARK

by Rose Mary Boehm

This collection is dedicated to Jane Pamenter, my guardian angel.

Contents

Part 1 – Imponderables

All That Remains

A murmur of atoms
taking off in graceful denial
of their former bonds.

Résumé

I was born to oils on canvas.
Mother was one of the whores of Ferrer-St. Denis,
painter of nineteenth Century Paris nights.
When I fell out of the womb I must have broken.
I am a hunchback. My father,
obsessed with women and paint,
tried to kill me with a palette knife.
My mother fled the studio,
leaving behind the afterbirth and
one shoe.

What regrets I have are not for my untimely
and unseemly birth, but for my genius.
When that knife nicked my baby skin,
oil paint and turpentine entered my veins.
There is nothing I can't paint. I smell the colours
and feel the lines in my belly. I rise in ecstasy
on light and shade, on this daub of red (the life-giver),
or a brilliant white (the lace maker), or a multitude
of greens the origins of which I've never seen.

One day my mother forgot me somewhere.
I was picked up by the wife of a mediocre
painter who soon made it to fame
and wealth. Put me to work when I was five.
Art historians everywhere sing his genius.

The Cretan Witch

Zene was born on Crete. The sailor
Dimitris had brought her to Cyprus, his earth.
In the village they all recognized her for what she was.
Had she not plucked Phokas' son from certain death?

Next she'd danced. An offering to the old gods.
When young Yorgos made eyes at her daughter,
Zene had looked at him. When he died of the fever,
she had picked up a chicken by the neck, sliced off
its head with the knife she always carried
in her apron's pocket, and bathed her
wooden doorstep in the gushing blood.

Today she wears the big black dress made from silk
for the holy day when they remember
the dead. Tables bend under the weight
of *kolifa, haloumi* and black olives.
Today is the day of All Souls.

Dreaming of Prometheus

My legs are stretching
towards the horizon.
My head is huge. I follow

my eyes as they bounce
towards the sea over red sand.
I am growing and begin to fill my
world. Water is rising. Through

my feet into my belly, into my lungs.
My heart on a stick above
the castle walls. I sit below,
watching. The orange sun

is eaten by a huge bird, wing-feathers
pointing fingers. It drops down
fast and swoops towards my heart.

First a stabbing pain and then I'm
ingurgitated. Fused we fly
to meet the man who stole the fire.

Daphne, Apollo's Sacred Laurel

*Apollo was about to catch the nymph, when she called upon
her father, and he cast upon her an enchantment of great power,
her skin turned into bark, her hair became leaves, and her
arms were transformed into branches.*

The green hill stretches its large wings.
Just off the summit, leaning windward,
the one tree prepares for takeoff. A lone bird
pecks at its steel-blue feathers in distress.

Fingers of bark close over her breast,
a dryad combs her hair to leaves while
her arms, thinning and hardening, reach
upwards in despair, her feet rooted
while stumbling onwards.

In Daphne's paradise the shepherd rhymes
in G-minor. The notes fall gently
on her translucent skin, then burrow themselves
deep into her essence.

Soft calls for rescue float free off her lips
but no-one will come to her aid today.

Philemon and Baucis

Snow on the iced-up steps
bits of slate broken,
a frozen rabbit skin dangled
from a hook near the door.
Come in, come in, you can't
stay out there. This weather
is meant for bears
and even they are hibernating.

Snow piled high at the back
cutting the light, frosted glass
with elaborate designs. A fire
in the open grate. She buzzed
about the small kitchen
excitedly wiping her hands
on her apron. A mug full
of steaming coffee.

Dad, come and see what
the storm brought in. A big
old man bent under the arch
when he entered the kitchen
from the other room.
He chewed and smiled
and sharpened his axe.

All Hallows' Eve

This moon is rough around
the edges.
It's a humble tumble fumble moon.

Santa Muerte.
Dance of those who know.
Who've been.
Samhain.

Beat the rhythm with the bones. Bring
back the cattle.
Lawter.
Day of slaughter.

Santa Muerte, the night walker stalker
out
about.

Sindhe doors.
Light the good fires.
Set a table for dead kin.
Prepare the barn.

Black clouds obscure the gallows
hallows
holy be your offering.

Smoke soak my skin,
ablute, restitute, retribute.

The Night He Stopped Being a Boy

He stands for a while,
hands in his pockets,
touching the secrete stone
from the midnight pond
under the rain trees.

His cap pushed to the back
of his head, stubborn stubble
brushes up from his scalp.
His trousers reach almost
to his knees, his shoes
sturdy, his imagination
limitless, his fear palpable.

Testing himself against trees,
ferns, undergrowth, night birds,
rustlings, and all things that wait
behind the dense shrubs
to taste his flesh.

He is not at all sure
he'll see his mother ever
again, but he knows that
something is watching.

Witness

From my terrace I watched
them roll up the lawn, shrink
the trees, pack away the roots.

What used to be parked cars
were waiting
as neat metal parcels.

A huge dark beast exhaled,
melted the asphalt,
slurped up the road.

On the horizon the sun sizzled
and sank, making a hole
which the ocean quickly filled.

Heavy clouds lifted junk,
trucks ached uphill
and someone switched off the stars.

Waterways

The green girl waited at the pier.
Hovered around the black pylons,
wet and rotting, lashed by the waves,
painted in abstracts
by sea moss.

Fernando pushed out his boat.
Young, brown, muscular and carefree.
The birds screeched in anticipation
of his return. Sea lions pretended
not to notice. Nets neatly rolled,
ready for an early winter catch.
Oil lamp in the bow.

She slid into the *lancha*. Undulated,
coiled beneath the tackle. Weeks later
they found him washed up on the beach
near turtle rock, a smile on his blue lips.

Dover to Canterbury

We'll soon pass the spot where I
see her every time. Not once has she missed.
Started to call her Emma.

The rain whips against
smeared windows. I strain
to peer into the night.

Perhaps she had bathed in
the arrogance of wealth,
the handsomeness of knowing
her place. Couldn't have been
more than about twenty-five.

One day I ask in the pub.
Drive to the estate.
The manor and grounds hidden
behind a gnarled, leafless overgrowth.
Scale the crumbling wall.

An anemic light from a dying
autumn moon haloes a woman. I follow.
Her long hair barely catches the weak light.

Her white gown billowing in the breeze
she hovers near the train lines.
Sparks spew into thick black.

A locomotive riots closer and bucks
when brakes screech it to a sudden
halt. In glowing white a woman
lies under the unforgiving wheels.

I tried to rescue her one hundred years
too late. But she knew I was watching.

Epilogue Found in the Diaries
of the Widow Rochester

(*Jane Eyre by Charlotte Brontë*)

Yes, reader, I married him.
A short while after our son was born
his obsessions began, and I recognized
his first wife's despair. Edward, even though
no longer completely blind, did not ever fully regain
his sight and distrusted the world and me.

My marriage became darker and darker
until I reverted to calling him 'Mr. Rochester'.
At moments it was as though a beam of sunlight
filtered through the curtains of foreboding
and I would take heart, only to be plunged
once more into the deepest gloom. One starless
night Mr Rochester fell off his horse and broke
his neck. Since then guilt has been my companion
and melancholy covers me like a heavy blanket.

Still, I can hear my children playing under the trees.
Occasional laughter drifts my way. We are blessed.

Another Mermaid Story

A small, brown village
on the Cornish coast.
Ruby married Fred.
She'd had enough of filing
in the 'Museum for Fishing and Smuggling'.
Fred liked Ruby because she was round
and sleek as a seal.
A slight scent of ocean
hovered over her skin.

Ravenous triplets sucked her dry.
In the supermarket she pushed
a tank with three activated
missiles from aisle to aisle.

Ruby soon neglected them.
Preferred to watch
the silvery catches
in the harbour.

Fred hired a nanny. Took to her.
Ruby took to the fishermen.
Both grew into the comfortable
co-existence of mutual dislike.

Ruby disappeared.
Fred drank her health.
In the bar that night a fisherman
mentioned that he'd seen a selky
swim out into the Celtic Sea.

Waterbodies

Ship with sails cut from red-poppy, fat
with the breeze. Those who wait.
The bloated bodies blue below. Chimneys
throw out shabby sheets, marigolds flutter
on the wings of *mariposas* while the white
whale sings its *cante jondo*. Grass trumpets
and lily bells, the source flows from
red leaves, cool Narcissus bends
over the still, green waters, the eyes
of roses take us to the edge of the world.

foundations

cracks
in concrete walls
held up by graffiti
passing trains
shake foundations
pale humans
huddle in corners
with devices that
promise memories
of things never known
and whisper
on a wind charged
with a wild fragrance:
don't deny the old gods

Earth to Earth

Told you to leave me alone. Look the other way. Don't pull me out of the fire, don't get me off the hook, don't rescue this here lamb from the wolves. Once my flesh has been burned away, I will have an idea of why I should avoid the fire next time. Once I opened my mouth to try and catch that shiny, moving object and it has lodged itself into my upper jaw, the other end of the hook protruding through my left eye, I shall avoid those spawning rivers. Once I have lain with the rascal wolf and he has eaten my heart I shall be alert to the danger of the hunter. Look the other way. Why else did I commence this blood journey but to experience the joy of pain, the enslavement of lust and the overcoming of fear. You will be found pressed between the pages of moldy ancient tomes. Parchment to parchment.

Very Near Where the Birches Grew

Something lives by Nedderston bridge.
Not on land, not under the overhanging
branches of the weeping willow,
but in the dark water.

Where we used to hang out to learn
about fear, where we shrieked and splashed
in the fast-moving rivulets, where we imagined
the trolls and faeries falling on us
from the willow's confusion,
where sunlight barely reached the soft,
squashy cushions woven from water plantain,
and sweet flag, and big blue stem.
Something is following us.

You probably think I made it all up, or perhaps
that I am a true witch's daughter.
Don't be so sure.
Look now and you'll see the dark outline
of a small, shaggy, undulating shape
moving silently below the water.

Swamp Woman

In slow-moving waters swamp woman makes her home.
Swamp children are born in the flower of water lilies,
rocked to sleep by the toads on giant lily-pads,
dragon-fly formations their entertainment
and taught by the bespectacled cayman.
There's no land like wetland.
When swamp woman passes
she exudes the odor of mold and rotting wood,
there is a greenish tint to her skin
which is too large for her body.
She lives in splashes of recognition
and the word 'drainage' for her means death–
which is ninety percent certain.

Damage Control

Four damaged dolls
and I lived in my house.
My mother knew, but
I failed to find my affliction.

There were five damaged
lovers in my life. I failed to see
how loving could have
cut them so deeply.

My children brought each
a piece of me into this world
and, in despair, changed into toads.

I often squat in the mud by the pond
learning a new way to speak,
especially with my daughters.

The Woman Who Won't Take a Lover

The afternoon slowly trickles between
her spread fingers, over her forehead,
into her closed eyes. She lets herself sink
to the floor, onto her knees.
Hard wood, splinters, rusty nails
mark her flesh.

An insect buzzes, thuds against
the dirty window pane.
Today she feels equally
trapped. No wings or vision.
Dust motes settle.
She is still.
Head bent.

From the park children's summer voices.
A goldfinch in the nearby pine.
The clock's pendulum's familiar rhythm.

Nothing has her attention
except the swelling of her lust.
Barbed wire cuts into her upper thigh.
A drop of blood congeals.

The Soothsayer

'Sooth', a word conjuring up
my mother's breath and the smell
of milk and that soft-hard warmth
under my hands.

The woman said I had been a man
in my previous lives. Said this time
around I was practicing to be a woman.
Said she saw a sword at my left hip.
(My left leg is stronger than the right
and shorter, and my sword arm
had an easy time holding my babies.)

And you, my lover, so unsure of where
your life lies, were inflamed by the thought
of the woman who would have been a man.

The Secret of Creation

Last night I designed a large forest with many strange beasts.
I snapped my fingers and it changed before my eyes
into an army (each soldier a waking tree), flat tanks,
and a fat general who rolled a howitzer
into position. He indicated I should stand aside.
I didn't wait around to see what would happen next.
Instead, I floated, feather-light and misty,
into a garden filled with butterflies powdered a metallic
hue of blue. They rose as I landed, looking at me with
astonished eyes while pulling up their undercarriages.
Passengers in each one of them. A goat ate the grass roof
of my house. No longer sure who I was so I invented you
to confirm that I exist.

A Deluge by Any Other Name

Tell me the story of the deluge,
sleep-mate of the anaconda,
shaman of the Urarina,
the downstream people.

Tell me about the first,
the one who climbed the cudí tree
and saved himself when
the daughter of the ayahuasca god
pissed a flood after the festival.
His wily wife also clung to the tree,
became a termite nest.

You can't give your true name, but
all of nature knows it after you've
looked deep into the bottomless
Angel Trumpets.

Slash and burn.
Slash and burn.
The white faces got weeds for corn.
The Amazon was on your side.
So you let down your guard.

You never knew
your enemy's true name.
Roundup. Glyphosate.
Noisy gods with wings fly overhead,
misting death into your green immensity.

After the Floods

Relentless programming of blood sacrifices consumes
the halcyon days of summer. Autumn gold hides
behind blind transom windows and hoary doors.

Transient bitterness settles in the dark, squishy roots
of inducement. Turning lazily in the river waters,
swollen wooden shapes hint at their former integrity.

Colliding fronts squash floating stars, giving
no inducement to those who would stay.

Amazonia

When the dog's front half disappeared
under a heap of soggy leaves, I kicked
away that mix of rotting vegetable matter
and saw it. Man, I smelled it. It made
curious humming noises and something like
the sound bubbles make when they burst.

Decomposition, they call it. When the dog
had calmed, we just stood there under the giant
ferns. From the nearest kapok hung a termite
nest like a tumorous growth as large as a backpack.

Flesh had again become part of the earth. No CSI
in Amazonia, no cell phone connection, no 911.
Man or beast, who cares.
Just matter to be reabsorbed.

Depths

At five-thousand meters deep I see your absent dance,
pale blue with emerald lining and hundreds of beaded frowns.

You refuse to open your petals to me or to the morning dew;
the night flyer's plumed feelers probe the lips of your deep.

When you lie dreaming in the darkest well of fathomless waters,
do not light up for the passing voyeur who may well
sever your stem.

Beware of those who would join your clouded voyage
across space time,
pick wanderers who can measure the transparencies you weave.

You saw me across miles of ocean floor and bade me farewell
while countless floating diamonds knitted you a veil of forgetting.

Night of the Cayman

His smile is coated in frost
which makes his mouth glitter.
The pole dancers gyrate
timidly when he enters.
The lap dancers scurry like roaches,
disappear under the floorboards.
His golden snake-skin boots have
heels that fit wherever he decides
to engage. Black, oiled curls hide
eyes that cut.

The hunter catches his prey
with one swift movement.
His teeth are red.
Where he is not,
fiery sparks seek dry tinder.
He wades through the slimy
edges of stagnant pools. Knows
where to find his quarry.

In the sleepy marshes his armor
has rusted. Silently the knife
slides into the soft between his ribs.

Between Here and Midnight

Walking along the Pacific coast
night comes upon us abruptly.

We sit and watch the last hot ore
dipping into Prussian blue.

Flames are dying behind
a black wall of insubstantiality.

Giant footprints fill with red lava.
Overflowing.
Alluvial.

These angels have large beaks,
the wings of black swans.
Comfortable on the foam of roaring
waves, they set fire to the sea.

Close my eyes, go inward, back to a time
when I was shaped. When I promised
the old gods that I'd heed my own advice.

Promised I'd remember the dead
and watch the robin.

The smelter of all that is
tried me and spat me out.
I am not about to become
indignant.

Consequences

Willow, wicker, wicca,
binding birch and ash
on witches' brooms.

First to leaf, the last
to lose. Water seeker.
Accessory to earth's
rainment, worshipping
nature's bones of stone.

Wanted to know who danced
to the flute while you slept
through the death time of winter.

One primordial morning
your memory showed you
the sacred hazel, invoked
by poets and seekers.

You asked him to be spared
the shedding until he grew tired
of your begging.

Do you know now? No flute,
no dance. Just winter's
unforgiving hold. Frozen
your gesture of seeking favours,
you lost your power of giving.

Fear of Fire

Alone I am like a dry twig.
Good for lighting fires. Sparking
so easily, brighting so gloriously.

The man who passes by the brook
at the bottom of the large meadow
every afternoon. Will he search

for my crackling gift at sundown?
Will he hear me snapping under
his heavy boot, glad of the sound?

He finds me and sees how bright
I burn. I shall ignite and kindle, scorch
and incinerate. He'll not contain me.

Alarmed, he throws me
into the stream,
from where I rise,
soft and fresh, filled
with vital juices.

I know the perfect place for kindling,
for consuming flames before the dowsing.

Phoenix

The whites of many eyes flash behind
a dense forest of steles. An echo
confuses the careless passenger

with 10,000 years of voices
and contemplation riding on the wings
of the sacred vulture; diving into

the abyss with the falcon and
soaring with the nightjar, his nasal
boom calling the ancients.

Birds' protective powers hovering
over pharaohs and gods alike could not
prevent their descent into Amenta

where souls are preparing
for the fire of rebirth.

Collector of Days

An old man. Stooped. A black suit, cardboard collar.
A grey beard, glasses over sad, sunken eyes.
A much-fingered wooden box. An old, dark shop.
Antique clocks, hesitant chimes.

The old man buys days; dog days,
death days, murderous ones...
The day a woman caused her lover's death,
the night a father witnessed his daughter's suicide,
the afternoon a mother helplessly
watched her small son drown,
the day the earth stood still.

All come to him to sell their worst days.
And nights.
Twenty-four hours.
He takes them off their hands.
He guards them in the box, cherishes
the treasures it contained. Strokes it
gently before he settles for the night,
but he doesn't sleep. His clients forget
their transaction. Man and women wonder
where Tuesday has gone, Monday,
Wednesday, or Friday, or why the matron
down the road is dressed up
to go to church on a Saturday.

Emptiness accompanies the collector.
His clocks ring hollow.

The light stops at the dirt-covered
windows, his hunger never sated.
Some days cannot be bought.

A Form of Destruction

I watch you in your den. The dust
of books and parchments settling softly
on grey. You hold the linen tester close.
Pagan text on human skin, scrubbed off
Wiccan codices and other heresies.

You first gathered my pages,
then sewed me at the central fold.
A palimpsest overpainted with new
icons. A book overwritten with lies.

When you were done with me, I could not
re-write myself. Got lost in the faintly
legible remains gnawed by mice, pecked by beaks,
used as breeding ground by assorted grubs.

I now think of myself as no more than a curiosity,
an ancient vellum over which acolytes
and old priests masturbate.

Starting Over

Old and dusty, fusty.
The librarian in Babel.
First, letters drop from a turning wheel,
then words. Collecting all that's sacred
before the towers crumble. After all,
words carry the weight and mass
of extinguished suns.

The vulture allows the updraft to lift it,
finds dead languages and carries them
to its tome-lined nest.
But that is tomorrow.

Leather-bound books grow from ancient
burial grounds reaching for the light,
falling open on crumbling pages.

Parchments extol the virtue of silence.
When the quiet never ends
we know we are falling,
unencumbered by syntax.

Revert the wheel,
take back the words
to the beginning.

In a Straitjacket

Tunnels without air.
Droplets of night sweat
roll like mercury. Merge
with the brook

at the bottom of the iron
leg on a creaking bedstead.
The white iguana extends
his five long fingers and closes
his eyes. Feeling his way

along my thigh. The angel
with wooden wings claps
on the green mosquito net.
Turns back, aims its long beak
at me. Storks bring babies,
do they not?

The fevers came early this
year. Where are my arms?
The face that stares
through the almost
opaque windowpanes

is divided into small pixels.
Morning is nothing here
and the moon barge hangs
somewhere on that branch

grinning like the Cheshire Cat.
The iron grids promise permanence.

A Trip

You are cold.
Broken a little.
Bruised everywhere.
Try and sleep. You ache. Consider
your options. Scream.
The fuzzy edge of the moon.
Soon
you have light for a few
precious minutes.
You have become transparent.
You drift off.

When you wake you remember
and begin to untangle your wings
from the green web. In the unquiet
waters ripples my face and you know
who betrayed you.

A Man of Iron

He's held together
by invisible wires of will,
tendons straining under the command
to hold at all cost,
not recognizing death
in which he won't believe.
Stretching out next to his pale love
in the bed made of white shrouds,
he gives her one last kiss,
his warm breath forcing
his conviction into her flat lungs.

A Bell Rings

but whales no longer pass in August,
the end of summer when moon escapes
from the black hole, and seven orphans
enter into complex negotiations
with the outward-bound behemouth. Economy
Class. Near the engine room.
Plangent and suffocating.
Heat and fire.
Your shiv's viscid consummation
lets her wake on a bed of liquid rubies.
Don't look back
or you will turn to stone.

The Jigger Variations

I
On the right track but not streamlined.
You were wiping imaginary sweat
from a brow permanently furrowed.
Should have resisted the temptation.
Marriage a metonym for failure.

II
Buried your head in my flesh,
a hungry beast that feeds on warm,
pulsing blood, prepared to loose
its life in return for sustenance.

III
You were warming your hands over an open fire
down by the embankment.
Your cup—measureless measure.
The night was cold, the fire uneasy.
Bubble bubble.

IV
Sails set. No doubting the direction.
Storms subsided.
A deep breath puts distance between
acute distress and foreboding.
Spray. Salt in my eyes.

Portent

The pharaoh's dream:
seven ears of corn
blasted by the east wind.

Moses summons the east wind
to bring the locusts
and to part the Red Sea.

The east wind.
Destruction of the wicked
called forth by God himself.

Mary Poppins arrives
carried by the east wind
and will stay
'until the wind changes.'

Sherlock: 'There's an east wind coming, Watson.'
'You left the East Wind to me,' said Gimli,
'but I will say naught of it.'
'That is as it should be,' says Aragorn.
'In Minas Tirith they endure the East Wind,
but they do not ask it for tidings...'

In 'Bleak House', Mr Jarndyce
refers to the east wind:
'I am always conscious of an uncomfortable

sensation now and then
when the wind is blowing in the east."

Genghis Khan: the east wind
that changed the map of the world.

Torment

We are circling black holes, dancing
around magnets that attract
half-cooked memories, hints of pain and pleasure,
burned wings on the way to the sun.

Sweat on skin against skin, staccato breath,
pumping, compulsory, doomed.
Bonding or simple pleasure?
The cry. Love hurts.

The dog howls at the hunter's moon.
Foe or friend? In answer to the song
of that orb which moves our waters?
There is ache and longing.

Noise, voice, ringing on Sunday mornings. Church bells,
hells bells, come to worship, worship, worship. Money
and good works, the pastor in his black gown counting
the coins. His face shines in the light of stained glass.

Black cigars with wings. Droning the long buzz,
raining apocalypse. Red skies at night.
Don't make me go into the dark
alone. Sister Emilia is praying. She has no rosary.

Wave to the Moon

Warnings ignored and whole islands disappeared.
Coastal cities graves for those who thought
this was a hoax. Our last refuge,

the city in ruin in the middle of a water-bound nowhere
that can no longer sustain us. Yes, we know. Yes,
we dance. Yes, we sing the songs all but forgotten.

Goodbye, sun. Goodbye moon.
You look down on our demise, indifferent.
We are about to return to the element

from whence we came. Somewhere, humans
are developing gills and fins only to be rejected.

God About His Actions
(Overheard Sound Bite)

Smiting was fun for a while, but soon there
were too many of you. And leave Nietzsche
out of this. He was one of the worst blamers.
Job did all this to himself, the bonehead,
and then blamed me. Thinking he knew
what I wanted of him. I wanted nothing.
Just wanted him to shut up. Thought
if I emptied the cornucopia of my benevolence
over him he'd be too busy counting his sheep.

Immersion

So they're going to baptize them. Greek
Orthodox. I never really believed. Figured
it was up to the adults to decide the name of their god,
the smell of their incense, which ring to kiss.
But there's something to be said for 'belonging'.
Congregation. Family. Group. Herd. Gaggle.
Religion. As long as the little ones don't mind
being dunked. All that oil all over the place
and the priest murmuring and mumbling
benedictions (I hope), the icons scaring you
witless. Their eyes follow you everywhere.
When I consented to offer my daughter on the altar
of medieval ritual, she carried the mark of fear
for the rest of her life. She thought herself
caught in a macabre practice of Satanism.
Believe in one, believe in the other. The old
grandpa from a village in Cyprus was happy.

Sacrifices

The gods tire of sacrifices.
I'll light a candle, Holy Virgin.
Just give me what I want.

You're standing at heaven's
door with a sledgehammer,
but when the gods aren't looking
you sneak in.

Tortured and bruised
you wail: What kind of god
allows this to happen…

What would a god want
with the blood of a lamb?
Your prayer is tainted
by the stink.

Sacrifice a virgin
on the altar of ignorance.
Throw one of the crew
into the maelstrom to save
the ship.

Build a pyre
for the heretics.
Burn the feet
of the new priest.

Sister Emilia

She'd herself danced with the devil.
So she said.
Over and over again.
When she pulpiteered about Lucifer
a wistful smile seemed to weave itself into her
face, even gentled that huge hooked nose.
Made the rimless glasses sparkle.

On Sundays she wore a frozen smile.
The wolf ingratiating himself to that little
lonely girl in the woods, his head covered
by a starched, white coif.
Leaving room for the ears.
Under his chin the big white bow.

Sin, sinner, sinnest.
A basket full of gluttony.
Lipsticks made from damnation.
Lust, iniquity, transgression, sloth.
Wrath.

Snow White and seven castrated dwarfs.
Virgins are eaten by dragons.
King Kong the gentle, imprisoned and
exhibited, prodded and cut.
Edification.

Hallelujah.
In the name of the Lord.
When Sister Emilia stopped preaching,
her face bathed in holy sweat and zealotry,
I imagined how she once took money before the service.

Sunday School

He said it would be our secret.
When he touched me there
it hurt and made me feel
like when Josh and I played doctors
behind the tool shed.
And he said it was God's will;
because that's what girls are made for
and who best but him to teach
me how to pray in the right position.
When he pulled down my knickers
he said he just wanted to see
whether the devil
had already made himself at home.

Church Choir

Too small
to carry the cross.
Too young for anything
but a mended gown.
The skufia falls
over my ears.
Let me be one of them.
Let me sing like them.
Let me fit in.

The pastor is huge.
I can see the hair
in his nostrils
when he says that
Alfred May was a good man.
Spittle flies.
I wipe my face quickly,
just in case.
He's lying. I know.
That man kicked my dog.

Hand over hand
they lower the coffin.
Handfuls of earth plop
onto the wooden top.
The hymn assures us,
"See the Light!
See the Sun!
I'm just going home..."

Doubt it. I think
He's down there
in the dark.

If There is a Next Time

Next time I shall not wait
for the lion, not be bruised
by exaltation. I shall be the stalker
of the female deer, my quiver full
of silver arrows glinting
in anticipation. At night
the owls will sit on my shoulder,
the moon itself will hide
behind poison clouds
of redemption.
There will be a feast
for the fallen, and manna
in the desert, multi-colored coats
for the undulating strays
to make them visible
from a great distance.

I'll be the bridge
across the fiery cataclysm
and a light house for those
whose shadows disappeared
in the starless black of countless nights.
I'll refurbish the house
of my fathers. No-one will be able
to enter without a password.

What If

inspired by David Eagleman

1
You get to your afterlife and God
has gone AWOL – visiting his friends
downstairs. Nobody cooks for anybody,
the angels are worn out, thin
and grey. Even the clouds look shabby.
The harps have lost their strings.

2
You get to your afterlife perhaps
and you find out why you were on earth
in the first place. There was something
like a gas leak in heaven and some
had to be evacuated, losing their wings
while they waited to be recalled.
Angel Administrativo had lost the
little green book in which our names
were written in red. In the kitchens
they steamed it as green veg.

3
You get to the afterlife and realize
that you never left at all. You were
dreaming again, and that car crash
woke you up. You wonder what happened
to all the others who pretended thereness.

4

You get to your afterlife. The windows
are barred, gardens overgrown, an
undernourished dog with matted pelt
lies panting under a rotting porch.
You call. There's only an echo.

Part 2 - Embers

The Signs Were Here All Along

Weak light, black earth frozen
hard. Pale days during which
the birds lost their voices, not daring
to give away their positions, lest
they too would suffer the blight.
Lines undefined, dull mornings
eating their advance through
the dim undergrowth, aimless
living bows at breaking point.
My boots find no purchase,
the ground iced suddenly,
my ankles fold more than once.
I can't break the fall, my body
slides forward, I don't trust my eyes,
but my hands bless the impossible; hidden
under the briars unfolds an act of faith
and sheer perseverance: the first
snowdrops pushing out of the frozen
womb, insisting it's their time.

English Spring Sunday

We met at the station
and drove into the shire.
I'd forgotten how green wet green is.
Talking, catching up –
it's been a year.
Wasn't really worth opening the brolly,
the rain came softly from all sides.

The pub, dark and low-ceilinged.
Right by the canal.
A fire lit.
Steak-and-kidney pie and a pint please.
We had planned to sit in the garden
watching the boats idling by.
Still, it was good.

At the next table sat foreigners
with loads of kids
all in brightly coloured slickers.
They said they were Finnish, had hired
a longboat for the weekend.

The tallest and blondest said, smiling,
We have a heat wave in Finland right now.

Another Spring

In those last days, boys in uniform
came past the house where mothers
would fit them out with their son's trousers
and shirts —the weather had turned mild.

In those last days I didn't sleep a child's
sleep. We'd shuffle to the shelter
that smelled of cool earth, moisture
and things growing on wet walls, settle

into the night counting the seconds, minutes
from the first droning. We waited
for deafening obliteration. I shivered
and crept further into my blanket

when we heard the bombs make contact,
the staccato of strafing fighter planes—
the *flak* had long since made a vow of silence—
and boys using bazookas

on anything that moved.
On one of those last days my brother
pushed his teddy between my praying hands
and I found solace in worn tufts of wool.

Heimweh is More Than a Flesh Wound

Geography is not important.
Everywhere
is the operative word.

Bared soul.
Barefoot.
Bare.

Tread carefully.
Mind your underbelly.
Be a turtle.

Carry the essence
in your hold all.
No roots allowed
past the security check.
They can see with
their X-ray machines.

You carry
a sharp, merciless
switchblade
made of stainless
grief.

Jazz Breaks My Heart

Swinging on the blue notes
getting stung by alterations,
drowning gladly in the chase,
leaning back into the groove.
I hear the inner voice
fragmented between the bass
and the break, lost in fusion.
Melodic minor harmonies
render me helpless.

Before the Storm

The old black artist is dying in his turret in North London
where for over half a century he painted Shostakovich.
The walls have absorbed music fused with acrylics.

I wind wreaths for princes without castles,
those who use paper bags for helmets.

Gods shape universes
from broken shrines.

I lost you because
I wasn't there.

'Moonlight in Vermont'

Vermont took on a special shine
on the small dance floor
just off the famous Boul' Mich.
Your feet were as large
as your frame and your height,
and my face rested on your
starched shirt front. I was afraid
I'd smudge my foundation (tone Biscuit)
and you'd be appalled. But then
you'd just stolen two crystal droplets
from the hotel's chandelier
and threaded those old wires
through the holes in my earlobes
with some pomp. I didn't expect
a starched dress shirt from
someone called Bill.

Fishing

We pretended to fish
with first morning light,
the waking leaves
and early birds, the stillness
of Dutch waters.
Jumping fish
startled us.

Your call conjured up
damaged enchantments.

I have this space
deep inside. Something
buried alive,
still writhing
when dawn breaks
an unquiet night.

Though you got old,
you knew
that we'd been lovers.
The strain in your voice
told me you remembered.

clandestine

meet me at the old
victoria station hotel
make it eleven.

hookers, lovers, trains
pass sooty windows

don't bring luggage
just remember
how I loved you
last winter in Antwerp.

your wet skin reflects
the almost light
under these high ceilings,
bent venetian blinds hide
curtains torn by time,
the station clock
has no mercy.

Ashes

I stood naked, reflected
in your eyes, dark as storm clouds.
On the edge of that cheap
hotel bed you, beast of prey,
ready to go for the kill.

Through the breaking, slatted
blinds the viscous southern sun played
on our bodies. A cockroach with wings
watched from the ripped jute
that once covered the wall.

After the boat had taken us back
across the lake you kissed my forehead,
left me there. Had to visit your mother.
A brass band began to play.
I didn't watch you go.

Half Remembered

In the cornucopia of my life
none of the pain remains.
The scabs have healed
and disappeared.
That's proof enough.
But I cannot recall a single hurt.
The knife that cut deep,
a film before my eyes.
Yet the years erased the ache,
except for that soft pressure of your hand
just where my neck and shoulders meet
'steering' me along the Rue du Bac.

East West

He had the voice.
There was the accent.
That Hebrew 'r', pronounced
in the throat.

When he played it was
for her, she whose bed
he had left only an hour before.
Shaving, the 'monkey suit',
packing his violin
into the old case
his mother had bought
when she made
him go to lessons.

The old violin professor.
The old piano teacher.
The old chess champion.
Those who had escaped.

He stroked her with his
'r's, he caressed her with
his smile, he pizzicatoed her
with his fingers, he sat
naked on the bedside table
in a hotel which had seen
better days. A faun playing
Bach's violin concerto in A minor.

He said he'd play it for her.
Like Cinderella she lost
her shoe. But the prince
never found it in the dark.

Nostalgia

I'm happy here; and yet...
a cloud in passing
smiles at me the way this urchin did
in Umbria and, over there, that rock
looks like Thierry, his Gauloise
glued to his lips;
the humid heat
reminds me of Chiang Mai.

Pacific sunsets do not conjure
the frozen Baltic or the milling crowds
of Oxford Street; no image
takes me to the Brenner Pass
or to the glorious anemones
of Aphrodite's meadows dressed in spring.

I see the snapshots in my mind.
Why does one image stay and others fade?
Did I leave marks in alien eyes,
or footprints in the stony coast of Cork?

For Sale

On Google Earth I can see
our old van rusting in the yard
and the profusion of honeysuckle
that smothered us with loveliness.

The huge green roof of leaves
is the walnut tree. I know that beneath
it is a bench on which it used to drop
its missiles every autumn.

The termites we ran out one by one
until we discovered a weapon
of mass destruction.
There was some guilt.

When I had breakfast with the wasps
in the fig tree, I knew I belonged.

Then the grapes rotted on the vines
because the gypsies didn't
turn up for a bumper harvest.
We slipped on fallen olives.

During monsoon-like downpours
every hole in the roof filled our buckets
with rainwater and us with a hard kind of love,
until the tornado ripped a huge branch
from the apple tree leaving an open wound,

and the peach tree broke under
the weight of its fruit.

One day the well ran dry.
Time to move on.
All that's left is the letter box,
leaning forward like an old, broken man.

About High Heels

In the streetlights' orange hues, every-day items
are shadows against the walls, exotic and possibly
threatening. The Pacific's regular breathing flows
over me. Going on eighty, very little disturbs me now.
The peace of knowing it's not forever.
Memories come unbidden.

Peep toes, red, heels three-and-a-half inches.
Brings out the calf. Tightly cinched trench,
ponytail whipping. My feet hurt. Click-clack.
If he could see me now.
The fifties, a time when women push out
pointed breasts from under tight sweaters,
when blue is never worn with green; baby pink
and baby blue the latest that Spring.
Sleeping with metal rollers under plastic caps,
a natural deterrent to casual, short-lived
relationships. The same clothes cannot be worn
to the office lest people talk.

Werner borrows his father's Merc on Sundays.
His soft, feminine hands on the steering wheel,
his nails a tad too long. Blond hair falling daringly
over one eye, quotes Gottfried Benn.

Oval Egyptian cigarettes, no filter. Lighting
them for him at seventeen, addicted smoker
at seventeen and a bit, date raped at eighteen.

Finally I stop reminiscing and fall asleep,
smiling to myself.
I own five pairs of comfortable shoes.

Having a Beer in the Canoe Club

The tables and benches are wet.
Barges on the Rhine low their mourning.
Water stands high after the rains.
On the opposite bank, the sharp
chimneys of the steelworks entertain us
with reflected-light swordplay. As far
as we can see the meadows are empty,
bushels of grass on mounds above the alluvium.
We lift our glasses. A solitary canoe
is berthing at the jetty.
I don't have fibromyalgia, you say.
I have cancer. And the silence changes
colour and our eyes won't meet.

When Your Ring Became Too Large For Your Finger

I thought girls can't whistle. Something to do
with their teeth perhaps, with the shape of soft mouths.

Girls couldn't build kites either, I thought, or fly them
with the skill required to keep them up there
until everyone else had given up. Girls couldn't wear
trousers. I too wanted to stick my hands deep inside
pockets and find pebbles and elastic rings
from mother's fruit conserve jars.

My trousers now have deep pockets, but the flying
is done in machines with metal wings and big jet engines.
You used to stand there, faithfully, outside
the customs gates, one hand buried in your coat pocket
as though digging for that last frog, one hand waving
at your little sister who was wheeling her
Samsonite. It was always only for a short visit.

Yesterday your son picket me up and tried
to tell me that my six-foot-four brother weighed
160 Pounds. You smiled, pulling back skin over
predator's teeth, and I tried not to think
of how you used to span sandwich paper
over balsa wood wings of model planes
which will never fly again.

School Reunion

Fifty years later we meet again.
The 'in'-group found me via the internet.
I travelled all the way from Spain.

Once I was friendly with three or four.
As close as you get when you
bike to school together.

The boys used to wait for us
under the plane trees,
showed off their hands-free skills.

I didn't remember their names,
30 old men and 40 old women,
pot bellies, sparse hair, shapeless

bodies in serious suits, lips cut
across wrinkled faces.
One wheel chair.

I avoided the mirror when I left.
One old man, leaned against the fence,
holding his face in his hands.

Aunt Martha's Adornments

She hobbles to her place at the table
squinting to read the names
on those large gold-rimmed plates,
too vain to pull out her glasses.
She was invited for old time's sake.

A big brooch on her lapel leads the eye
away from her wrinkled neck, her long earlobes
pulled down by gold. Dramatic rings
emphasize knuckles and thick veins.
You don't see the liver spots
when the rubies are real.

A choker with an ivory pendant
moves up and down when she swallows,
hardly able to chew her meat. Hair curls
over a neck which was once kissed in the nape.

She remembers young, smooth skin
on round forearms, bracelets tinkling,
silver rings on delicate fingers,
a turquoise pendant leading the eye
to her rounded breasts, rhinestones
shimmering in the candlelight.

How could she have arrived here from there—
it seemed only yesterday when he pretended
to strangle her with her Indian silver chain.

The Old Women of Saxony

They sat, their legs open, their floral
skirts falling between. Aprons. Always
something to do in their hands, a bowl
resting on their thighs, knitting needles clicking,
picking peas from the pods. Hands with calluses,
broken nails, black furrows. Grey hair
pulled into buns, the hairs that remembered
their girlhood curling over wrinkled ears.
Steel-rimmed glasses, except for Auntie Helen
who had the eyes of a hawk.
No adornments.

And girls they used to be. Sepia photos
on the sideboards, the girls with their men.
The girls coquette, their young men stiff,
looking straight into the camera, in uniform,
next to their girls, not touching.
That was before the First War.
They never came back, and the old women
were left to their sisterhood.

They worked the land. Brought in
peas, potatoes, beans from their gardens.
Chickens, a fearsome cockerel, warm eggs.
There was the occasional rabbit a nephew
had trapped.

They loved us with harsh voices, rough hands,
with berries, apples, and home-made jams.

Hard they were, these women. Unafraid.
Had seen the worst. 'We said it when Hitler
was alive and we say it now we have
the Bolsheviks here. All the same anyway.
What more can they do to us—
shoot us?' And they smiled.

We escaped to the West. They couldn't
come out, we couldn't go back.
Survived well into the 50s.
There were their letters.

Waiting

The others talk about death. How they
held their father's hand. Hard of crying.
How their Mother smiled one last smile when they
saw who it was, who'd come from far away
to accompany them on that last stretch.
How their sister, brother took their
last breath in their arms, how their lover
walked away, collar up against
the night air, how their dog
expired under the lorry,
how the dead cat came
home in a box. Some 'lost' their
children to the unforeseen, others
watched their comrades explode,
there are those who buried wives
or husband.

Death has touched me only from afar,
took some figures off the board,
left some holes in the fabric
of my life, blanked out colours, drew
misty curtains over faces, made me
a murderer: there were
the goldfish that froze in the pond,
the hibernating hamsters buried
in the back of the garden. Whenever
I imagine old friends, I correct myself
quickly: they're probably dead.

Being as a migrating bird,
I have held nobody's hand,
didn't listen to any last, laboured breathing,
did not sit on plastic-covered chairs
in the hospital ward of last resort.
I have not been a witness.
Yet.

Acknowledgments

ATTICUS: Having a Beer in the Canoe Club, VATAR: Résumé; Dreaming of Prometheus. AVOCET: English Spring Sunday. BLACK POPPY REVIEW: The Cretan Witch; Daphne, Apollo's Sacred Laurel; Very Near Where the Birches Grew; Consequences; In a Straitjacket; Dover to Canterbury; Night of the Cayman. BLUE NIB: Foundations; Aunt Martha's Adornments; Make-believe. BROADKILL REVIEW: A Bell Rings; Jazz Breaks My Heart. BURNING WORD: Philemon and Baucis; *Heimweh* is More Than a Flesh Wound. CRACK THE SPINE: Earth to Earth; Sacrifices. EUNOIA: For Sale. GALWAY REVIEW: What If. GINOSKO: A Trip; Portent. GOODWORKS REVIEW: Half Remembered. KIND OF A HURRICANE PRESS: Between Here and Midnight. INK, SWEAT & TEARS: We Didn't Know We Were Poor. KIND OF A HURRICANE PRESS: The Signs Where Here All Along; MISFIT MAGAZINE: The Secret of Creation; Collector of Days; Sunday School; Before the Storm. MONTERRAY POETRY REVIEW: If There is a Next Time. MUDDY RIVER: The Woman Who Won't Take a Lover. NAPALM & NOVOCAINE: Fishing. NAUGATUCK RIVER REVIEW: The Old Women of Saxony. NINE MUSES: Church Choir. OFF COURSE: All That Remains. PIRENE'S FOUNTAIN: Phoenix. POETIC DIVERSITY: Waterways. POETRY QUARTERLY: Torment. PUNCHNELL'S: Sister Emilia. PYROKINECTION: Ashes. RAW: A Form of Destruction. RED RIVER REVIEW: East West. SAN ANTONIO REVIEW: Wave to the Moon; When Your Ring Became Too Large for your Finger. SBLAAM: Depth. SILVER BIRCH: All Hallow's Eve; Epilogue Found in the Diaries of the Widow Rochester; Moonlight in Vermont; . SHOT GLASS JOURNAL: The Soothsayer. STRONG VERSE: Amazonia. TOE GOOD: The Night he Stopped Being a Boy; Witness. TURTLE ISLAND: Waterbodies. UNDER THE RADAR: About High Heels. VERSE-VIRTUAL: Waiting. WILDROOF JOURNAL: A Deluge by Any Other Name. WRITER'S BLOCK: Another Spring.

www.ingramcontent.com/pod-product-compliance
Lightning Source LLC
Chambersburg PA
CBHW031211160726
47992CB00006B/2688